Little People, BIG DREAMS
MOTHER TERESA

Written by
Mª Isabel Sánchez Vegara

Illustrated by
Natascha Rosenberg

Frances Lincoln
Children's Books

Once, there was a little Albanian girl who was always willing to give a helping hand. Her name was Agnes, and she lived in Skopje, with her parents and two siblings.

Agnes was raised to love God and love others above all else. Little did she know that in the future she would be known as Saint Teresa of Calcutta...

One day, a new priest arrived in town. He had been working in India, far from where Agnes lived. She loved listening to his stories about helping the poor in the city of Calcutta.

So, when she turned 18, Agnes said goodbye to her family and started a long journey. She was determined to become a nun and help people—no matter what.

She traveled to Ireland and joined the sisters of Loreto.
Once she had settled in at the convent, Agnes asked the
nuns to call her "Teresa" from that day on.

A few months later, she was ready to board a ship and travel to India. The language, the colors, the food, the smells...everything was new and different for her!

Mother Teresa taught at a school for many years.
But she knew there were some people who needed
her more than her students: the poorest of the poor.

Mother Teresa took to the streets of Calcutta, determined to help the first person in need. She had hardly taken three steps before she stumbled upon a woman who was lying on the ground.

Soon, 12 students joined her. They called themselves the "Missionaries of Charity," and they set out to care for all those who needed it. They chose to wear a simple sari.

Mother Teresa opened a hospital in an old Hindu temple. There was always one more bed, one more plate of rice, and one more blanket to cover whoever needed it. She knew that the smallest things could make the biggest difference.

For more than twenty years, she picked up thousands of people from the streets of India. She opened hospitals, orphanages, and schools all over the world.

She received all the awards that could be given to a single person. But she only accepted them in the name of the poor.

Mother Teresa sent a beautiful message out to the world: it doesn't matter if you do big or small things in your life, as long as you do them with great love.

MOTHER TERESA

(Born 1910 • Died 1997)

c. 1925 (left)

c. 1930

Anjezë Gonxhe Bojaxhiu was of Albanian descent and born in
Skopje (now the capital of North Macedonia). The Anglicized version
of Anjezë (Agnes) has been used in this book. Agnes lived with
her mother, father, older brother, and sister. Her family followed
the Roman Catholic faith, and this could be seen in their everyday
life. Her family wasn't rich but opened their home to people who
needed help. Her mother would provide strangers with hot food
and a place to rest. She taught Agnes to see God in the faces of
strangers. At 12, Agnes then heard "the call" to dedicate her life to
God. Her mother thought she was too young, but the voice persisted
over the next few years. Agnes was fascinated by stories of Catholic

1971   1974

missionaries, people who traveled to faraway places to help those in
need. At 18, she set off to join a convent in Ireland, taking her vows
as Sister Teresa. She traveled to India to teach at a school in Calcutta,
where she became "Mother Teresa." Mother Teresa was on a train to
Darjeeling when she heard "the call within the call." She believed God
wanted her to help the poor while living among them. She founded
the "Missionaries of Charity," and many nuns joined her. They set up
hospitals, comforted the sick, and cared for the poor when no one else
did. She was awarded the Nobel Peace Prize in 1979 for her work. After
she died, she was awarded a sainthood by Pope Francis, in 2015. The
Missionaries of Charity still continue Saint Teresa's work today.

Want to find out more about **Mother Teresa?**
Read one of these great books:

Who Was Mother Teresa? by Jim Gigliotti and David Groff
DK Biography: Mother Teresa by Maya Gold
Mother Teresa: The Life of Mother Teresa by Paul Harrison

You can read more about the work of the Missionaries of Charity, on their website: The Mother Teresa of Calcutta Center.

Brimming with creative inspiration, how-to projects, and useful information to enrich your everyday life, Quarto Knows is a favorite destination for those pursuing their interests and passions. Visit our site and dig deeper with our books into your area of interest: Quarto Creates, Quarto Cooks, Quarto Homes, Quarto Lives, Quarto Drives, Quarto Explores, Quarto Gifts, or Quarto Kids.

Inspiring | Educating | Creating | Entertaining

Text © 2018 Mª Isabel Sánchez Vegara. Illustrations © 2018 Natascha Rosenberg.

First Published in the UK in 2018 by Frances Lincoln Children's Books, an imprint of The Quarto Group.
400 First Avenue North, Suite 400, Minneapolis, MN 55401, USA.
T (612) 344-8100 F (612) 344-8692 www.QuartoKnows.com
First Published in Spain in 2018 under the title Pequeña & Grande Mother Teresa
by Alba Editorial, s.l.u., Baixada de Sant Miquel, 1, 08002 Barcelona
www.albaeditorial.es

ISBN 978-1-78603-230-0

The illustrations were created with gouache, colored pencils, scanned textures, and digital techniques.
Set in Futura BT.

Published by Rachel Williams • Designed by Karissa Santos
Edited by Katy Flint • Production by Jenny Cundill

Manufactured in Guangdong, China CC082020

9

Photographic acknowledgments (pages 28–29, from left to right) 1. The young Albanian born Anjez Gonxhe Bojaxhiu, with her sister Aga, in Macedonian traditional costume, c. 1925 © Vittoriano Rastelli / Corbis via Getty Images 2. Mother Teresa of Calcutta, c. 1930 © Vittoriano Rastelli / Corbis via Getty Images 3. Mother Teresa sighted on October 16, 1971 © Ron Galella / Getty Images 4. Mother Teresa with a child from the orphanage she operates in Calcutta, 1974 © Nik Wheeler / Sygma via Getty Images

Collect the
Little People, BIG DREAMS series:

FRIDA KAHLO

ISBN: 978-1-84780-783-0

COCO CHANEL

ISBN: 978-1-84780-784-7

MAYA ANGELOU

ISBN: 978-1-84780-889-9

AMELIA EARHART

ISBN: 978-1-84780-888-2

AGATHA CHRISTIE

ISBN: 978-1-84780-960-5

MARIE CURIE

ISBN: 978-1-84780-962-9

ROSA PARKS

ISBN: 978-1-78603-018-4

AUDREY HEPBURN

ISBN: 978-1-78603-053-5

EMMELINE PANKHURST

ISBN: 978-1-78603-020-7

ELLA FITZGERALD

ISBN: 978-1-78603-087-0

ADA LOVELACE

ISBN: 978-1-78603-076-4

JANE AUSTEN

ISBN: 978-1-78603-120-4

GEORGIA O'KEEFFE

ISBN: 978-1-78603-122-8

HARRIET TUBMAN

ISBN: 978-1-78603-227-0

ANNE FRANK

ISBN: 978-1-78603-229-4

MOTHER TERESA

ISBN: 978-1-78603-230-0

JOSEPHINE BAKER

ISBN: 978-1-78603-228-7

L. M. MONTGOMERY

ISBN: 978-1-78603-233-1

JANE GOODALL

ISBN: 978-1-78603-231-7

SIMONE DE BEAUVOIR

ISBN: 978-1-78603-232-4

MUHAMMAD ALI

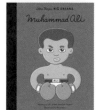

ISBN: 978-1-78603-331-4

STEPHEN HAWKING

ISBN: 978-1-78603-333-8

MARIA MONTESSORI

ISBN: 978-1-78603-755-8

VIVIENNE WESTWOOD

ISBN: 978-1-78603-757-2

MAHATMA GANDHI

ISBN: 978-1-78603-787-9

DAVID BOWIE

ISBN: 978-1-78603-332-1

WILMA RUDOLPH

ISBN: 978-1-78603-751-0

DOLLY PARTON

ISBN: 978-1-78603-760-2

BRUCE LEE

ISBN: 978-1-78603-789-3

RUDOLF NUREYEV

ISBN: 978-1-78603-791-6

ZAHA HADID

ISBN: 978-1-78603-745-9

MARY SHELLEY

ISBN: 978-1-78603-748-0

MARTIN LUTHER KING JR.

ISBN: 978-0-7112-4567-9

DAVID ATTENBOROUGH

ISBN: 978-0-7112-4564-8

ASTRID LINDGREN

ISBN: 978-0-7112-5217-2

EVONNE GOOLAGONG

ISBN: 978-0-7112-4586-0

BOB DYLAN

ISBN: 978-0-7112-4675-1

ALAN TURING

ISBN: 978-0-7112-4678-2

BILLIE JEAN KING

ISBN: 978-0-7112-4693-5

GRETA THUNBERG

ISBN: 978-0-7112-5645-3

JESSE OWENS

ISBN: 978-0-7112-4583-9

JEAN-MICHEL BASQUIAT

ISBN: 978-0-7112-4580-8

ARETHA FRANKLIN

ISBN: 978-0-7112-4686-7

CORAZON AQUINO

ISBN: 978-0-7112-4684-3

PELÉ

ISBN: 978-0-7112-4573-0

ERNEST SHACKLETON

ISBN: 978-0-7112-4571-6

STEVE JOBS

ISBN: 978-0-7112-4577-8

AYRTON SENNA

ISBN: 978-0-7112-4672-0

LOUISE BOURGEOIS

ISBN: 978-0-7112-4690-4

ELTON JOHN

ISBN: 978-0-7112-5840-2